LATE RETURNS

A MEMOIR OF TED BERRIGAN

BY TOM CLARK

WITH 11 LETTERS
FROM BERRIGAN
TO THE AUTHOR
AND 20
PHOTOGRAPHS
OF BERRIGAN
AND FRIENDS

TOMBOUCTOU
1985

© 1985 Tom Clark

All rights reserved. For information address Tombouctou Books, Box 265, Bolinas, CA 94924.

Acknowledgments:

For permission to reproduce a selection of Ted Berrigan's letters to Tom Clark, thanks to: Alice Notley Berrigan; Frank Walter, Fales Librarian, Elmer Holmes Bobst Library, New York University; James Davis, Head, Department of Special Collections, University Research Library, University of California at Los Angeles; George Butterick, Curator of Literary Archives, Wilbur Cross Library, University of Connecticut. All photographs in this book are from the collections of Alice Notley Berrigan and Tom Clark. Special thanks to Peter Schjeldahl, who took many of the early photographs.

Cover drawing by Tom Clark.

Designed by Stephen Emerson.

Typography by Rock & Jones.

Also available in a limited, signed hardbound edition from the publisher.

ISBN 0-939180-35-9 (trade paper edition)
ISBN 0-939180-38-3 (signed hardbound edition)

CONTENTS

Late Returns: A Memoir by Tom Clark   11
20 Photographs of Berrigan and Friends   57
11 Letters of Ted Berrigan   67

LATE
RETURNS

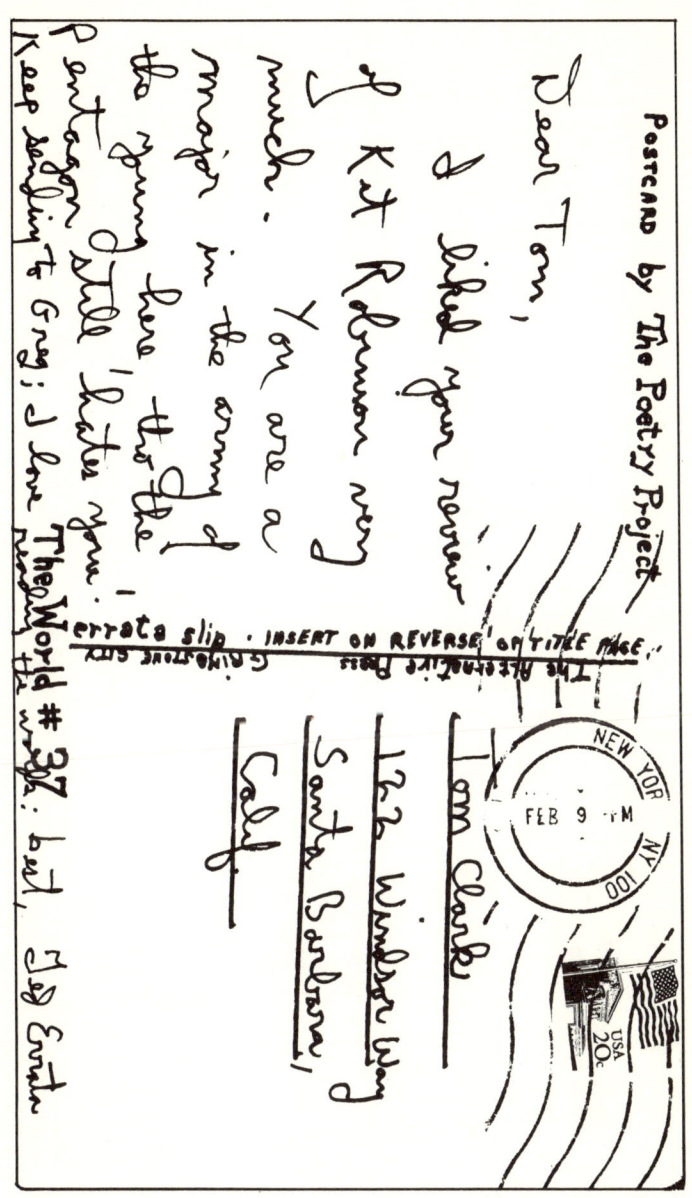

Photostat of a postcard from Berrigan to Clark, postmarked February 9, 1983.

LATE
RETURNS

A MEMOIR BY TOM CLARK

y original acquaintance with Ted Berrigan came, appropriately, through his work, which I first encountered early in 1965, when I discovered those arresting Lower East Side mimeo magazines *C* (edited by Berrigan) and *Fuck You: A Magazine of the Arts* (edited by Ed Sanders) in Shakespeare & Co., a bookstore in Paris. I was staying in a borrowed apartment on Avenue Mozart, and one day, hiking across the city to the Left Bank apartment of another visiting American poet, Robert Bly, I stopped at Shakespeare's, and browsing there, found these magazines, which proposed a kind of writing — and an approach to life and experience — so radically dissimilar to those I'd previously pursued that I felt the boards shake slightly under my feet as I stood and read amid the quiet shelves.

This first taste of the new American street prosody had the powerful effect of making it hard for me to take quite so seriously Mr. Bly's own earnest literary magazine, *The Sixties*, of which I received a fresh copy later the same afternoon.

Back in London, I walked into Better Books on Charing Cross Road and found a new issue of *Art & Literature*—the first issue, I think, of that magazine—containing two of Ted's sonnets. These are the first Berrigan poems I remember really focusing on. One of them was Sonnet LXVI. It began: "it was summer. We were there. And THERE WAS NO/ MONEY..." Who else said things like that in poems? A few lines later, a B-29 was "plunging to Ploesti." Then came sailboats, "trembling velvet," tears, vernacular ejaculations, aesthetic admonitions, all leading up to a final "semblance of motion, omniscience." This little tour de force conjoined literal verisimilitude ("I am closing my window") and democratic vocabulary ("like sittin' ducks") with international-style linguistic bravado and sheer nerve. Even more surprising, it somehow hung together as a poem, and *worked*. Unprepared, my first impulse was to dismiss it as a mere fluke. But those B-29's kept on plunging through my word-memory into "the sea, which is dark, cool, and green," for weeks afterward.

A year or so later, Ed Dorn blew into England like a lean

breeze off the great American plains, carrying with him—among other pieces of news—a set of tapes of the recent Berkeley Poetry Conference. Berrigan and Sanders had read at Berkeley, as "new voices" nominated by their superiors (Ginsberg, Creeley, Olson, et al.) for the occasion. I subsequently learned that it was at the Berkeley Conference that a young woman named Angelica Heinegg (whom I later married) first met Ted; characteristically, his greeting to her (at a party at Tom Parkinson's house) included the surreptitious slipping of a note down the front of her dress. Reading it at the first opportune moment, Angelica found that Ted had written, "Meet me outside in ten minutes!" At the time, she considered the note simply a good-natured bluff; later, however, after getting to know Ted better, she concluded that it had probably been a good-natured, serious proposition. Ted had a great appreciation of the virtues of women, and at that period it was not only a spectator's appreciation but, whenever possible, a participatory one.

Ed and I sat in Ed's office on the new campus at Essex, smoked hash-and-tobacco joints, and dug the Berkeley tapes. They contained many great moments, but to me Ted's reading was the central revelation. On the tape his voice had a tense edge to it, probably bred of a combination of nervousness—this was his first California reading and, if the ominous audience silence in the wake of such challengingly belligerent lines as "I like to beat people up" was any indication, was rather standoffishly received—and amphetamine. But as the reading wore on, it seemed from the tape that Ted's speed and heart were winning over a difficult crowd; an encouraging word from Robert Duncan was audible at one point. Ted read at length from *The Sonnets*—"baffling combustions are everywhere!"—capturing all of that sequence's flowing, shifting, soft-focus layering of meaning and feeling; and also performed the comic masterpiece "A Personal Memoir of Tulsa, Oklahoma/1955-1956" ("There we were, on fire with being there, then/And so we put our pants on/And began to get undressed...") I'd never heard poetry sound so funny and so true at the same time; more important, the Americanness of the humor, smacking of a collision between the spirit of Will Rogers and modern pharmaceutical consciousness, struck me as an absolute relief after two years in the midst of English academic institutions, where the speech I'd been hearing had little relation to the speech I *knew*. The latter was very much present in Ted's reading, moving and jumping to the tune of a new kind of comic surrealism that sounded, I thought, like a message from the immediate literary future. Something was happening over there across the water and though I wasn't sure what it was, I knew I wanted to be a part of it.

I wrote to Ted asking for poems for *The Paris Review*, of which I was then poetry editor. He sent "works" (as he called all writings in poetry or prose) by the bunch—his own, and collaborations with other writers (Ron Padgett, Dick Gallup, Tom Veitch, Bernadette Mayer, Peter Schjeldahl). In rolled big chunks of his enigmatic cowboy novel, *Clear the Range*, composed by crossing out and replacing words in a pulp Western, as well as dozens of poems. I printed two Berrigan poems, that exuberant "mystery play" about a childhood Christmas, "Presence" ("and I am lost in the ringing elevator"), and one of the early sonnets, "The Fiend" (also about Christmas, and "keeping Christmas-safe each city block" in the city's "solid blooming winter") in *The Paris Review* #37—which, appropriately, bore an electric-bright green/red/yellow abstract Christmas tree on its cover.

The generous overflow of Berrigan poems and collaborations, as well as many works by fellow New York poets whom he'd alerted about my interest, went into the series of "one-shot" mimeo magazines (*Once, Twice, Thrice, Frice, Ice, Slice, Nice,* etc.) which I was simultaneously editing from the University of Essex. Many were the pill-bright, fluorescent-lit nights I spent alone in the empty institutional buidings, typing stencils, grinding the mimeo, collating and addressing envelopes to the hundred poets Ted was putting me in touch with. Watching my scholarly pursuits as a "research student" gradually give way to the production of live literature, my academic boss, Donald Davie, grew more and more restive, until one day he summoned me into his office to respond to a single chilling question: did I intend "to be a scholar or a Bohemian?" After riding the horns of that dilemma for about five seconds, I decided: neither! From that point, my days in academe were numbered.

Hitchhiking around the countryside to keep up with the Anglo version of the new poetry scene, I found plenty of British poets aware of the Black Mountain and Beat movements, but nobody who'd heard of the even newer poetry explosion going on in New York. Berrigan, Sanders & Co. were working with a raw American vocabulary which didn't suit the English palate. For information about their doings I counted on mail and visits by traveling New Yorkers. Aram Saroyan arrived and talked about Ted's psychedelic red sneakers (Aram, though, was already regarding Berrigan and Ron Padgett with a certain condescension, as interesting reactionaries unable to keep up with his—Aram's—own up-to-the-minute electric reductivism). Ron Padgett also showed up in

Essex, with news of his discoveries in French poetry (Reverdy, Max Jacob) and stories about the Tulsa days, when Ron, Dick Gallup, Joe Brainard and Ted had all been "on fire with being there." Donald Davie didn't know what to make of any of this. Ed Dorn was one thing, but Dorn was at least *serious*. When Davie asked Padgett a question about Idaho—a place where Davie had never been, but which he'd read about in Dorn's poems—Ron grinned and said that the only thing he knew about that state was that Judy Garland had been born there, in a trunk...a non-sequitur which left Davie stumped.

Ted's correspondence usually came in large, bulging envelopes, stuffed with amazing works. One of my favorites was his "Poem for Ed Sanders," which consisted of a single bold line, scrawled in huge holographic black capitals: "I AIN'T GONNA DIE." (I printed that one in *Thrice*.) What words could have better condensed the Berrigan philosophy of that era? A year or so later in New York, one tooth-jangling winter dawn as we were crossing 2nd Avenue on the way to Ted's apartment, he elaborated that philosophy for me. It's a moment I remember very clearly. He was wearing his Jim Bridger coat and toting a *New York Times* and a paper bag that contained Pepsis and donuts. (Along with the speed pills he gulped as other people swallow vitamins, sugar and starch were Ted's dietary staples.) Having been up all night as usual, we were both considerably strung-out at the moment, and our conversation had taken a serious turn, touching on the payment of one's dues in life—the rent, the gas and electric bills, and other basic debts. "What I tell 'em," Ted said, "is 'Put it on the cuff.' Like the airlines tell you—'Go now, pay later.' I believe in the Go Now, Pay Later Plan!"

"Put it on the cuff" was at that time one of Ted's favorite sayings, along with the Damon Runyonism, "Get The Money!" Both of them, of course, contained a heavy quotient of built-in irony. Ted never really got *the* money—only enough to last for today, or at best until the end of the week. And as he knew better than anybody, that score notched on the cuff steadily mounted up.

Re-reading Ted's old letters, it's evident I was sending him almost as many "works" as he was sending me. Which ones I sent, I'm no longer sure, except in those cases where Ted incorporated my work into his own—a habit of his which was also an important element in his compositional procedure, i.e. borrowing and then transforming other people's writings, in whole or part. (William Burroughs' cut-up method provided him with both model and excuse.) For example, I know I must have mailed Ted the manuscript of my 1966 novel "The Riot at the Garrick Theatre" (now lost; even I don't own a copy), since sea-changed swatches of it later turned up under the title "Gus" on p. 44 of Berrigan's Selected Poems, *So Going Around Cities*. And of course, he kept on sending me more and more work in return. Just before leaving England, I placed three of the best of *The Sonnets* in *The Paris Review* #40—the trio on the theme of "Fucking is so very lovely/who can say no to it later" (Sonnets LI, LII, LIII). These three, I've always thought, were very close to the center of the whole sonnet sequence—not only in the middle, but at the heart. *The Sonnets* was "an homage to myself" (LXXXVII) but also, equally consciously, an homage to love, full of living, breathing, rolling and tumbling sexual feeling.

I learned a lot about Ted's philosophy of life, before even meeting him, from reading *The Sonnets*, which contained a kind of composite self-portrait of the author—or at least his projection of himself. The modern, post-romantic art-hero, maker of big, perilous, splashy "major statements," was a persona that developed gradually between and through the lines. I later came to believe this was a persona Ted borrowed from Frank O'Hara, who'd developed it as a description of the New York abstract expressionist painters, those bigger-than-life figures who remained great heroes to Ted, as they'd been to Frank, his favorite poet. The lineage was evident. "But my poetry is *open*..." That openness, and the concomitant willingness to *pose*, without embarrassment, in the persona created by the poem, was Berrigan's inheritance from O'Hara.

For all its cut-up, plagiarizing, source-shuffling, commonplace-book quality, *The Sonnets* stated a singular philosophy. ("Meaning strides through these poems just as it strides through me." — Sonnet XLVIII.) It was a modular construction of personal mythology. The poems put forth a grandness of spirit, both as intent and in execution, that may have belied the economically pinched existence Ted was actually experiencing at the time, but certainly embodied the greater dimensions of his dreams, values and beliefs. Art and love were twin poles of the poem's whole compass. Poverty, pills and book-stealing were caught up in the major positive sweep of the work — as "problems" they were no more serious than mosquitos to Tarzan ("Je suis M'sieur Tarzan").

In an interview I did with him years later in Bolinas, Ted compared the compositional experience of being in the driver's seat, running the table, confident, flowing, strong, which he got when writing *The Sonnets*, with Arnold Palmer "charging" down a golf course on a beam of absolute certainty that every shot was headed straight for the hole. "I rage in a blue shirt at a brown desk in a/Bright room sustained by a bellyful of pills." Part of this sense of command, of course, was chemical—the gift of dexedrine, desoxyn, etc.—but a greater part was pure emotional largesse. "At night, awake, high on poems, or pills/or simple awe that loveliness exists, my lists/flow..." ("Words for Love"). The real subject of *The Sonnets* was the grand clarity of the moment of creation, something "stronger than alcohol, more great than song" (Sonnet III). The expansive, soul-inviting amplitude of the gesture ("Dreams, aspirations of presence!"—Sonnet XLIII) was as American as Whitman; Rimbaud and Juan Gris, Max Jacob and Apollinaire were in the poem, but only as honored guests. The resident legends were Ira Hayes, John Wayne, Davy Crockett, William Bonney, Jesse James.

In March 1967, I returned from England to the United States. I'd been out of the country nearly four years, a period in which America had been changing drastically—as, for that matter, I'd also done. The return trip across the water took a week, which gave me a little time to prepare myself for the sudden adjustment to this new state of the nation. The shock of arrival was enhanced by expectation and pharmaceuticals. I'd carried with me from London a small supply of pristine lab-produced LSD powder, the original pure variety, but as the liner entered New York Harbor it occurred to me that what with my long hair and pink-and-purple mod-madras jacket, I might draw the attention of U.S. Customs. So I loaded the LSD granules under my fingernails. Waiting in the 3rd-class bar for the ship to dock, I chewed my nails.

Customs inspection took several hours. The inspectors examined my trunkful of books with great care, pausing with special curiosity to leaf through the green-cover Olympia Press editions. By the time they'd finished, I was lit up like a pinball machine on Swiss acid.

At the Customs gate I was awaited by an entourage of writers with whom I'd established epistolary relations: Lewis Warsh, Anne Waldman, Peter Schjeldahl, Jim Brodey. After exchanging greetings we climbed into a taxi and rode to Schjeldahl's apartment on 3rd Street. The cab ride was one long hallucination: American traffic was huge, fast and honking! Everything looked bigger, faster and shinier than anything I'd experienced in years. At Schjeldahl's, a party quickly developed, even though it was noon on a Wednesday. Ted soon walked in: a big, lanky fellow (he was 33 years old) with long dark hair and a bushy beard, wearing baggy Army fatigue pants, a t-shirt and black horn-rim glasses. He was carrying a small vial of an amazing drug called STP. Rumor had it, this stuff was a mix of belladonna and printer's ink.

We mixed some with pot and smoked it in a pipe. Most of those present passed it up, but Ted, Jim Brodey and I took several hits. The experience was like instant poisoning. Blackout, head whirling, where am I? Then back down to the planet. But which planet? We gulped a few pills. I opened up my suitcase, pulled out my English psychedelic rock & roll records, like Jimi Hendrix's *Are You Experienced?*, and played them. After a while Lewis left to go to work, Anne followed; others drifted away. Ted, Jim Brodey and I moved out to dig the streets.

It was an unseasonably warm day, the sun was hot, spring was in the air. Color and noise everywhere. On 3rd Street, some black kids had a portable radio playing top volume: "Jimmy Mack" by Martha and the Vandellas. We walked all over the Lower East Side, Ted towing me from landmark to landmark. Jim Brodey tagged along for a while, then Ted forcefully hinted that we'd meet him later; Jim reluctantly cut off on his own. Ted wanted my full attention; this was the Big Introductory Tour.

Building by building, I learned everything that had happened on these streets, going back in history to the administration of Fiorello La Guardia. Here was where this painter lived, there was where that poet had written his greatest poems. We stood and gaped in awe at the 9th Street apartment where Frank O'Hara had resided. We cruised down Avenue B past Tompkins Square Park, Ted talking all the way. He led me up into Joe Brainard's tiny, austere apartment. Joe was drinking a Pepsi and working with nervous zeal on some flower paintings for his coming show at the Fishbach Gallery: big, splashy blossoms, inspired by the pictures on flower-seed packages. Quiet, polite, shy, but friendly, and obviously accustomed to Ted's visits, Joe offered us Pepsis, lit a cigarette, dutifully paused from his work long enough for Ted to deliver a little set speech on Joe's art.

We strolled back toward Ted's apartment, delving further into the East Side's jungle-like ethnic depths. Ted walked with a confident, long-striding swagger, elbows thrown out to command space, head cocked back and swiveling to take everything in: a chief surveying his territory. Every few strides he stopped to point out some significant aspect of the teeming streets. We paused at the Puerto Rican street vendors' stalls on Avenue C; Ted showed me where Joe purchased the religious bric-a-brac he employed in making his "madonnas" and grand "assemblages" (the largest of which, titled "Japan," was Joe's chef d'oeuvre, and could be viewed in Kenward Elmslie's apartment).

The Berrigan apartment was at 286 E. 2nd Street, between Avenues C and D, deep in the heart of the maelstrom. Three floors up, it faced south, with Ted's desk in the living room, next to a window overlooking Houston Street. The desk was loaded with books and typescripts of poems; on the wall alongside was a reproduction (evidently clipped from a book) of a daguerreotype portrait of Edgar Allen Poe. Here was where Ted sat and worked on poems, playing his typewriter hunt-and-peck style while his head rocked from side to side, giving the impression he was tuned in to a distant music (and certainly he *was*). Near the desk a small radio played Murray the K's rock & roll show on WOR—some of that week's songs were "Groovin'" by the Rascals, "At the Zoo" by Simon & Garfunkel, "White Rabbit" by the Jefferson Airplane. The walls of the small living room were lined with works by Joe Brainard, many of them "collaborations" Ted had had a hand in. The two small Berrigan children, David and Kate, slept in one of the two bedrooms—Ted jokingly called it "the orgy room," in honor of the big, crude, amiable pornographic frescoes by Lower East Side artist Steve Sunderland (author of the underground classics *The Banana Book* and *Sunlight in Jungleland*) which covered two of its walls.

Ted's wife Sandy maintained the domestic scene. They'd been married almost five years, Ted told me. Ted had gone from Providence College to Korea, where he served three years (1954-1957) in the Army, and from there to the U. of

Tulsa, where he enrolled as an undergraduate on the G.I. Bill. He picked up his bachelor's degree from Tulsa in 1959, two years later acquired an M.A. in English (specialty: G. B. Shaw), and in 1961 left for New York. The following year, on a visit to New Orleans where his friend Dick Gallup was briefly attending Tulane, Ted met Sandy, a Florida girl studying at Sophie Newcomb College. They quickly married, but on a subsequent trip to Sandy's home in Florida, the newlyweds met with serious resistance from the bride's parents; Ted was escorted out of the Florida town by local police. It took legal action to get her to New York ("in three hours I go to court to see if the world/will let me have a wife"—"Personal Poem #8").

Material difficulties were a commonplace of the Berrigan marriage. Ted rarely had any money, and making the rent was a constant struggle; stealing books for re-sale or bumming a few dollars from friends were extreme measures not unfamiliar to him. At the time of my arrival, Sandy was recovering from varicose vein surgery, working part-time, attending English courses at Hunter College by night, taking care of two youngsters, and providing tender loving care for her roaming poet-husband. Ted could be counted on to show up at home around dawn every day with at least enough milk and bread to provide breakfast for the kids. His own breakfast was a Pepsi and cookies or a Hostess Twinkie, delivered into his dark bedroom sometime after noon along with whatever mail might have arrived. He read, wrote, and ruled the home front while Sandy went to her after-dinner classes. By 10 p.m. she was usually at home; by 11, the kids were asleep, sometimes with the help of doses of paregoric. Ted was then released for his evening sojourn, which began with a stroll to Gem's Spa at St. Mark's Place and 2nd Avenue to buy the newspaper. From there he often continued to Anne and Lewis's apartment on the same block, where his presence dominated a nightly poetry salon that often continued until 2 a.m. At the Waldman/Warsh apartment Ted presided over the conversation and the record player, lobbying for songs like Dylan's "Visions of Johanna" and other favorite folk-rock tunes. Ted's musical taste ran to Dylan, Baez, Simon & Garfunkel, and Phil Ochs; among the British groups he favored the Stones and the Kinks; generally speaking he liked songs that carried some kind of substance or message in the lyrics. ("The rock & roll songs of this earth/ commingling absolute joy AND/incontrovertible joy of intelligence" — "Bean Spasms.")

Other regular stops on the Berrigan rounds included Peter Schjeldahl's and painter George Schneeman's apartments (at Schneeman's, he often served as the artist's model). Beyond

2 a.m., the rest of the night was Ted's special domain; his companions were those of his friends who kept similar late hours, which meant mainly the unmarried ones. Lee Crabtree, musician and Fug, was one of these. Once I'd secured my own apartment, I was another.

I spent my first few nights in New York sleeping in the Berrigans' "orgy room" with the kids, and accompanying Ted on his rounds. That first Wednesday evening we caught the tail-end of a David Antin reading at St. Mark's parish hall. Standing at the back of the hall, Ted delivered a comical running commentary on the poems for my benefit, simultaneously engaging a friendly lady painter with affectionate bear-hugs. Later in the evening he took me to a nearby loft to introduce me to that young woman's roommate, another painter, with whom Ted was conducting an ongoing romantic affair. She wasn't around. We went on to Anne and Lewis's, and eventually ended up around 3 a.m. at the apartment of a lady poet whose strong points, literary and otherwise, Ted had been enumerating at length as we proceeded through the now-vacant streets. Genuinely surprised to be awakened by two raving pill-heads at such an hour, the woman hesitantly opened the door to us, sleepily listened to Ted talk for about fifteen minutes, then kicked us out. Undaunted, Ted spent the long walk back to his house on a detailed exegesis of her behavior, and how it related to her character in general and to the universe at large. At the corner of 2nd Street and Avenue C we stopped at a small neighborhood grocery store, where Ted bought milk, bread, cookies and Pepsis. For him, it was just another day.

The next afternoon I got a taxi to move my trunk of books from Schjeldahl's apartment, where I'd left it, to Ted's building. Two friendly young hippies, one of them wearing a bright orange aviator's jumpsuit, happened to be stopping in at the Berrigans' that day. Obviously high as kites, they enthusiastically offered to help Ted and me trundle the battered trunk up three flights of stairs to the apartment. It turned out to be a job easier contemplated than performed, however. Two-and-a-half flights up, somebody's grasp slipped, and the trunk plummeted down the stairwell, hitting the ground-floor tile with a crash that sent books bursting out in all directions. A retired fireman who lived on the ground floor lent us some milk crates, in which we re-packed the books, and we carried them back up. This whole development delighted Ted, who liked the prospect of having a loose stash of interesting and curious books to pore over during the ensuing weeks while I searched for an apartment. To me, the comedy of the moving of the books came to symbolize the disorganization that seemed to invade my attempt at practicality during my stay in New York. Ted, who lived with and gloried in such disorganization, enjoyed the whole scene enormously, including my exasperation.

Finding an apartment proved approximately as easy as moving the books. After a few nights at Ted's, where things were crowded enough without me, I moved into Dick Gallup's apartment on 1st Street. Dick and his family, out of money and plagued by a continuous stream of robberies (every time they brought home a domestic appliance, it was stolen within 24 hours), had retreated to Tulsa for a respite from the trials of the city. During my stay, prospective burglars showed up at the door every few days, peering over my shoulder past the chain-lock, casing the place on the chance a new TV set had been bought (no such luck). The only vaguely stealable item I'd brought into the apartment was a vintage Magnavox phonograph, value about $5, and hardly worth the time of any self-respecting burglar. I, however, valued it highly, since I used it to play my Who, Hendrix, Kinks, Stones and Byrds LPs on. After a few weeks in New York, I went off to Chicago for a week. I left the apartment key with Ted. On my return, I entered the apartment to find the fire escape window wide open, and the record player and albums gone. My heart sank. I went over to Ted's to share my woes. It was late afternoon. Ted was in a great mood, feet up on his desk, drinking a Pepsi and listening to my Jefferson Airplane LP on the Magnavox. He'd come over to Dick's and picked it up to take care of it for me while I was away, he explained. Ted's philosophy always included the adage, "Mi casa tu casa." What was his was yours, and what was yours was his.

Eventually I found an apartment, one room on East 14th Street near Avenue B. The place had a hideaway bed, a dingy unlit kitchen containing a sink and a shower that didn't work, a toilet with a single blue light bulb, a non-functioning brick fireplace containing a huge bass drum bearing the inscription of a Polish neighborhood social club, and some cast-iron-and-wire book shelves that I'd found on the street. I lined the latter with books. They immediately accumulated a thick layer of the dust and grime that sifted in through the barred but screenless windows from the Con Ed plant on the opposite side of 14th Street. Across a courtyard, I had a view of an apartment full of Hare Krishna freaks. Downstairs, a bunch of Puerto Rican junkies stayed up all night doing a heavy trade in heroin and stolen goods, playing the same Wes Montgomery LP over and over. The landings and stairs were usually coated with puke. Upstairs, a young unmarried mother who didn't speak English was always breaking water pipes — my ceiling leaked, but I couldn't explain the problem to her. Through the walls, the powerful electrical system of the Chemical Bank (located next door) throbbed all night. Whenever you entered the apartment and turned on the lights, dozens of roaches scurried for cover. The rent was $60 a month. I lived there for a year, rarely going to sleep before daylight.

A couple of times a week, usually around 2 or 3 in the morning, Ted showed up, a bushy beard and horn rims looming fishlike through the peephole in my door, bearing Pepsis or coffee and donuts. We listened to records, talked, took turns at the old Smith Corona that I propped atop my reconstructed steamer-trunk, banging out collaborative poems. Of all the poems we wrote together—there must have been dozens—I've managed to save a copy of only one, something called "R.S.V.P.," written one freezing night "on the 3 a.m. shift." It must have been stormy out on the streets that night, because the poem contains a line that goes, "snow covers my calligraphic tracks."

I remember a lot of bleary dawns with Ted. We'd write poems, then walk out to dig the streets. Often we went to Tompkins Square Park, four blocks from my apartment. At dawn the park had a small population of speed freaks (we didn't consider ourselves speed freaks) and people walking dogs. Ted enjoyed digging the speed freaks. One warm spring morning a particularly bleak-looking speed freak approached us hesitantly. We said hello. The guy glanced around nervously, then handed us a brown paper shopping bag containing an injured pigeon, and asked us if we'd look after it. To my surprise, Ted said okay. The speed freak took off. We sat and discussed the problem for some time. What could we do about a pigeon with a broken wing in a shopping bag? Neither of us felt like taking it home. Was there an animal hospital nearby? Ted suggested we walk up toward 14th Street. When we got to 14th Street and Avenue B, a few steps from my door, I made it clear that I would *not* consider turning my apartment into a pigeon hospital. We turned west and headed for the all-night burger joint at 2nd Avenue and 14th Street. On the way we passed Larry Rivers' building. Ted suddenly got a bright idea. Larry had money, he'd be able to provide the pigeon with veterinary care. It seemed sensible enough. We delicately placed the pigeon next to the doorstep of the building where Rivers lived. Then we walked off to get hamburgers. We brought them back to my place, ate them, and considered what to do next. It was already fully light, around 6 a.m., too bright for poems. Ted, who'd taken more pills than I had, suggested continuing on to The Factory, Andy Warhol's uptown studio. Something was sure to be going on up there, he said. This seemed dubious to me.

Late Returns · 35

To convince me, Ted pointed to a reproduction of Andy's portrait of Liz Taylor, which I had pinned to the wall, and delivered a short lecture, something about its "electrical vibrations," as I remember. It's a genius painting, Ted said. Right, I said. Let's go up and dig The Factory, he said. No dice, I said. Ted rolled his eyes and made it clear I was not being a team player. Exhausted, all I could think of was hitting the hide-a-bed. What about that pigeon? he said. What *about* it, I said. Maybe we better check it out and see if it's okay, Ted said. It's got a bent frame. Fifty guys might be coming by and bothering it. I don't care, I said. Okay, Ted said. He left alone. The next time I saw him he told me he'd gone straight home and "slept fifty hours."

Ted had done a fake interview with John Cage. It consisted in part of lines stolen from an *Evergreen Review* interview with the Spanish playwright Arrabal, interspersed with joke lines by Ted plus additional passages taken from the writings of his friends, principally Dick Gallup. Cage was a great hero on the serious avant-garde scene, which was full of guys Ted considered slightly hilarious—like Dick Higgins, Allen Kaprow, etc. Ted wanted to spoof that whole scene. For instance, he inserted the question, "What do you think of Allen Kaprow?" "Allen Kaprow can go eat a Hershey bar!"

Cage answers. In another section of the interview, there's this exchange: "What kind of person was your mother?" "Very religious. Very. But now she is crazy. She lay on top of me when I was tied to the bed..."

Peter Schjeldahl published the interview in his magazine *Mother*. One day I was at Ted's when Schjeldahl phoned to say he had some incredible news and would be right over. About an hour later he arrived, in a three-piece suit, looking very nervous and disheveled. What happened? we asked. I got robbed, he said. They even took my umbrella. We expressed sympathy. People were getting robbed on the street in Ted's neighborhood all the time. It was no place to walk around in expensive-looking suits. Ted discreetly refrained from saying this. But what, he inquired after a certain calming-down period had elapsed, was this incredible news? Peter then informed him that both Ted and he (as editor of *Mother*) had been awarded $1000 government grants for the Cage interview, which had been selected as one of the year's best little-magazine features. The judge had been George Plimpton, editor of *The Paris Review*. This astonishing windfall came at a time when Ted was badly in arrears on rent payments. He was overjoyed and, for once, almost speechless.

Plimpton often threw lavish parties at his 72nd Street apartment. They were a pleasure to attend, since the quality of the food and drinks was very high, and the company was always interesting. George invited me now and then. Shortly after the magazine prize was announced, I went to a Plimpton party with Ted and Sandy. We also brought along two mutual friends, Lee Crabtree and Pete Kearney, both members of Ed Sanders' folk-rock group, The Fugs. (Of the five of us, Sandy and I are the only ones who are alive at this writing.)

The party was spectacular, as usual. In one corner, under a collection of George's autographed footballs, Terry Southern sat with a drink in his hand, surrounded by luscious teenage girls in mini-dresses cut about a foot above the kneecap. They hung on his every word. We Lower-East-Side types looked on in awe, munching catered turkey sandwiches. (Sandy filed about a dozen turkey sandwiches in her purse.) The party glided along. When not ogling the pretty women, Ted and I commented to each other on George's impressive collection of autographed bats and baseballs, team photos, etc. Then at one point, several drinks into the proceedings, I noticed Ted and George engaged in animated discussion. George was standing against a wall, next to his Detroit Lions team photo. He looked flustered. Ted was talking a mile a minute, the way Ted usually did. George was looking more and more upset. "You mean that whole interview was *made up?*" he was saying. "You never really *talked* to John Cage? You didn't even get his *permission?*" Ted was explaining that the whole thing had been a put-on, but that since it was done in the "spirit" of John Cage's "works," he was sure Cage wouldn't mind. George appeared to be at a loss for words. Once he fully grasped that he'd awarded a government prize for a bogus interview, he handled the occasion as graciously as possible. We all left shortly after that, and went around the corner to a dance hall in the East 60's where the Velvet Underground was playing. Anne and Lewis were there, so was Gerard Malanga. We all danced and joined Ted in laughing about how he'd pulled off his amazing John Cage caper.

The summer of 1967 was hot and dense. Many of our poet friends escaped to "the country"—Long Island, Vermont—for the summer. Ted and I spent most of the hot months in the city. I fell in with a hippie "tribe"—The Group Image. Psychedelic dances at Stony Brook and Palm Gardens, trips with Country Joe, trips with Everybody. On a trip to Woodstock for a music festival I rode in the back of a pickup truck driven by a couple of visiting Hell's Angels. In Orange County, state troopers stopped us; somebody had some marijuana, and we all spent a weekend in jail. The experience should have been "sobering," instead it was just unpleasant. Life went on. Grit and acid, strobe lights and cockroaches. Revolution was in the air. Abbie Hoffman, who'd helped me deal with the Orange County case, called one day and asked me to meet him on Sixth Avenue. I did. He asked if I'd like to take over the publishing end of the Comunications Company. I'd get a mimeograph machine as part of the deal, Abbie said. I considered this. Then he asked me how I felt about guns. The last mimeo publisher of the Communications Company had blown his head off. I wasn't sure what Abbie had in mind. I said no.

Ted and I attended the Grateful Dead's first New York concert in Tompkins Park. The New York *Daily News'* front page, the next day, featured a crowd shot from the concert. There among the zapped-out freaks were Ted (in horn rims and mesh t-shirt) and me (in shades). I later put the photo on the cover of a book of poems, called *Green*.

Neal Cassady came to town, burned-out and bitter but still talking up an electrical storm. The stoned denizens and tribal flower people of New York weren't sure what to make of him. Ted and I spent a night riding in a car with Neal and his girlfriend and a couple of hippie know-nothings. Ted dug Neal's rap—Cassady was one of the few men who ever out-talked him. The evening ended up at WBAI, the alternative radio station, Neal and Paul Krassner and Hugh Romney (Wavy Gravy) rapping while a lot of hippies pounded on homemade drums. Though he chauffeured them brilliantly, Neal didn't get along easily with the acid heads. He was of a previous generation, one that still communicated verbally. After a couple of nights in town, he was gone, pounding the Detroit iron back toward California.

I remember taking acid with Ted one night that summer and then watching old movies on TV at somebody's apartment—a roomful of purposefully nonverbal young people. The TV sound was off, and Ted provided exquisitely funny running commentary, supplying all parts of the dialogue. I hadn't laughed so hard in months. Everybody in the room seemed stunned, stupefied, as Ted's jokes spun past their stoned heads.

Ted was walking across Tompkins Park when some Puerto Rican kids jumped him. Unlike most of his poet friends (myself among them) Ted had never been hit on by street muggers. He was the Boss Man of the streets, never concerned about his safety, walking where and when he liked. This time, he had to run for it. He turned an ankle. It took him months to get over the whole experience, which unnerved him even more than it damaged him physically. The neighborhood was changing, new elements were coming in, everybody was high and some of the new elements were clearly very crazy. It was kind of a turning point for Ted. "White man, tomorrow you die!" After that, he started to exercise a little of the caution that he'd previously consigned to the uncharmed rest of us.

Jack Kerouac was a great hero to Ted. He'd been negotiating for over a year in hopes of doing a *Paris Review* interview with Jack. George Plimpton finally said okay. This wasn't going to be another put-on, Ted made it clear. Kerouac was also interested. His career in the doldrums, Jack hoped *Paris Review* coverage might revive it. This was the kind of "uptown scene" he'd always had trouble getting due respect from. Ted first proposed by mail that they stage the interview as a "Noh play." Jack hesitated about coming on too crazy— "Don't spoil my chances," he wrote back to Ted. Finally a conventional interview format was agreed on, but the date wasn't made firm. Ted decided to simply go ahead and try his luck.

Ron Padgett and I went along on the trip. Larry Bensky drove. We left one morning before dawn. By the time we got to Cambridge, all of us were drooping, except Ted. We spent the day in Cambridge with Aram Saroyan, who was living there. Riding on a sea of pills (Obitrol), Ted was primed to make this a Big Occasion. The trip gradually took on multiple significances for him. At the Lamont Library he turned up some Harvard *Advocate* poems of Frank O'Hara's which he'd never seen—a very positive omen, he thought. He also ran into an old girlfriend—another romantic resumption, further increasing the personal-myth quality and autobiographical importance of the trip for him. At the end of the day in Cambridge, he came back to Aram's place, sunburned, pumped-up, and talking a blue streak about his adventures. Ron and I, both weary, decided to drop out of the interview junket; clearly this was Ted's trip, we were extra baggage. Ted ran into Duncan McNaughton, who agreed to drive him on to Lowell for the interview. Correctly guessing that the son of one of Kerouac's favorite writers would be a useful presence on the visit, Ted persuaded Aram to accompany them. Ron and I rode back to New York with Larry Bensky.

Fifteen years later, in the course of writing a book on Kerouac, I wrote and asked Ted to tell me about the interview in Lowell. His response was a two-hour long-distance call from New York, recounting every detail of the visit. Jack had answered the door and invited Ted and friends to enter, but his wife Stella had quickly arrived and "started dragging him away," said Ted. "She said to us, 'No! No! Get away!' She was concerned about Jack going off on a giant bat with us." Once Ted had persuaded her the purpose of the visit was not a drinking party but a serious literary interview, Stella had relented, on one condition: "no drinks." Jack, however, nursed a bottle of his own throughout the visit. He seemed "a little down," Ted recalled, but only until Ted slipped him a few Obitrols. From that point, Kerouac grew more expansive and began to enjoy himself—"in many respects," Ted said, "due to the fact that I had slipped him those pills."

Jack "needled" Ted about his informal interview-style (and also about his "bad teeth," which Kerouac advised him to "get fixed"), but nonetheless answered his questions with "long speeches, using all his incredible voice stops and changes." After the interview, Stella gave Ted a tour of Jack's "impeccable" writing-room. Ted read for Jack a few sections of "Tambourine Life," and Aram recited some poems—"my arms are warm/Aram Saroyan." Then it was time to go. An uncomfortable moment: Jack wanted to leave along with his guests, "and go to a bar." But, said Ted, "Stella didn't want him to, and she really twisted his arm and made him stay home.... It was very touching, and very sad, because we were obviously taking the energy out of the room—there were three of us, you know, and we were *young*."

Back in New York, Ted made a transcript of the interview and began editing it with George Plimpton and Peter Ardery of *The Paris Review*. A disagreement developed between Plimpton and Berrigan over including some of Kerouac's remarks about literary homosexuals and his relations with them. According to Ted, Jack had said, "I got around a lot in my youth. I sat on a lot of couches with elegant young men in those days. You understand, Berrigan — blow jobs yes, ass jobs no!" Berrigan suggested to Plimpton that the remarks had been humorous and civilized. "It was Jack's statement in the face of all the things Allen Ginsberg was always saying about his sexuality," Ted proposed. Still, the remarks were excluded from the published interview (which did include some material inserted later after Kerouac had been provided further questions from the magazine, and had replied to these by mail).

Ted played the uncut interview tapes one night at Jack Boyce and Joanne Kyger's loft. A diverse crowd showed up, including Andy Warhol and several of his flunkies. The tapes contained much heavy-duty truth-telling that never got into the magazine — Kerouac raving at length about the perfidy of New York Jews, dishonest publishers, literary homosexuals, Communists, and purveyors of LSD.

Late Returns · **45**

In January 1968, I met my future wife at an uptown party Ted and I attended with Anne and Lewis, who were acquaintances of the host. It was a party full of young short-haired stockbrokers. One of them asked me sarcastically if I was "a member of the Byrds." My reply was to dance all evening with the prettiest girl in the room. Some weeks later this lovely young woman came along on a trip to Ann Arbor, where Ted, Ron Padgett and I were all to read our poems as part of a weeklong arts festival. We stayed in guest rooms in the Student Union. Angelica and I locked ourselves up in our room and acted like fiancées are supposed to. I remember Ted pounding on the door minutes before a scheduled poetry reading, loudly announcing, "You two are jeopardizing the future of American Poetry! Come out!"

Ted spent the days in Ann Arbor paying respectful homage to the ghost of Frank O'Hara, who'd written many of his early poems while in graduate school there. There was a memorial reading of Frank's poems, in which Ron, Ted and I all took part; Ted's reading was quite beautiful, and not without tears. One very cold day we all walked off campus to the rooming house on South University Street where Frank had lived. It looked like any other ordinary student rooming house on any other tree-lined street in Ann Arbor. We stood there shivering on the sidewalk, trying to share

Ted's glow of holy proximity-with-the-great. It was difficult. Not everybody has that sense of the immortality of poetry.

When we left, Ted stowed in his duffel bag a large desk lamp from his room in the Union. As we waited in the lobby for the airport limousine, Ted was obviously nervous. The officious young man who acted as liaison between the Union and the festival cast a few querulous glances at Ted's bag, which seemed to have grown substantially in size during the week of the festival. Ron Padgett, who has a highly developed sense of humor, gleefully noted Ted's discomfiture. The limousine came, we all left, and that was that. Back in New York, Ted installed the reading lamp in his bedroom, where it served him well.

Some weeks later, Ron wrote a letter to Ted on some stationery he'd taken from the Union. He signed the letter with the name of the young student liaison-man. In the letter, he charged Ted with stealing the lamp, and requested restitution. When Ted got the letter, he immediately wrote an anxious reply to the Union man, saying "I didn't steal that lamp!" Ron then revealed the joke to him. Furious, Ted vowed to get even. I don't know if he ever did. (His relationship with Ron always surpassed normal human understanding.)

In late March 1968, I got married in St. Mark's Church. Two days before the wedding, my apartment had been robbed and ransacked by the junkies downstairs. When I confronted them about this, they feigned remorse, but for the next two nights they kept climbing back up the fire escape to see if there was anything left to steal. It was time to go. After the wedding, I never went back to the apartment. I left what was there for the landlord to dispose of, and forfeited my deposit.

At the wedding, Ron was the best man, Ted gave away the bride. All three of us wore heavy wool double-breasted psychedelic gangster suits that looked like something left over from *Bonnie and Clyde.* These came from a poetry groupie named Shelley Lustig, whose husband ran a used clothing store. Not only were they similar to the outfits once worn by guys like Larry Fay and Frankie Marlow (from the Damon Runyon era), these may have been the *same suits!* Ted's was a grey three-piece pinstripe, worn over a dark blue shirt and white-and-green floral necktie. With his bushy reddish whiskers, he looked very colorful strolling up the aisle, the visionary bride in white lace on his arm. Poets David Shapiro, Dick Gallup, Larry Fagin, and the painter Mike

Goldberg (who'd provided my Italian wedding shirt) played and sang the wedding music during the ceremony. Afterwards, there was a party at Anne and Lewis's. In those few moments when he wasn't busy kissing the bride, Ted proffered upon me solemn paternal advice on my new condition as a married man.

The next time I saw Ted was in California, where my wife and I had gone to live. He visited Bolinas occasionally, staying with us at times, other times with Lewis and Phoebe MacAdams. (Both houses were on Nymph Road, which Ted mentions in talking about some familiar "walks" in the title poem of *So Going Around Cities*.) After one of his visits to the Clark household he sent us a poem "Things to Do in Bolinas," which indicated fairly clearly that the rural character of the place in those days wasn't quite suited to his urban sense of action. (His list of "things to do" included "watch the natives suffer... freeze & sleep... yearn for city lights.")

Nevertheless he did spend several long periods in Bolinas. One was in 1971, at poet Larry Kearney's house, where we did the "Ted Berrigan Interview" that later appeared in *United Artists* #4. Another time he spent several months with the MacAdamses. By the time of these visits he'd separated from Sandy and was living with his second wife, the poet Alice Notley, who'd been his student at Iowa. These extended Bolinas stays were somewhat a matter of duress; Ted had no money. I remember doling out books from my shelves for him to sell to book dealers in San Francisco. The money went for his pills and basic expenses. (One of the books which he *didn't* sell was Wordsworth's poems in the Oxford edition; he kept it and extracted from it the lines that made up his own poem "The Complete Prelude.") During his stay with the MacAdamses on Nymph Road, Ted and I wrote a whole book together, in prose and poetry, *Bolinas Eyewash.* I haven't had a copy for years. Ted once said it was about to be published by a press in Chicago. If it was, I never knew it.

From New York City, from Long Island, from England; from Iowa, Michigan and Chicago (he taught for a year in all three places, and whenever he'd taught somewhere, we later got visits from his students, many of whom had adopted his vocabulary lock stock and barrel), he continued to send letters and poems, many of which I put in *The Paris Review* and in an anthology I edited, called *All Stars,* for which Ted wrote his "Three Sonnets and a Coda: for Tom Clark." "Anti-War Poem," "Heroin," "Things to Do in Providence" (all printed in PR) were among the dozens of poems he sent. When he was working in colleges, he often phoned late at night from his departmental offices, and we talked as we had in the old days (cf. my poem "Locations," in *Air*). But the old days, of course, seemed to get further and further away. Ted's poems started to contain hints about "back death" and "the pills aren't working" and "I need to kill someone." Life never got easier. Though clearly there were still some pleasant moments, that score on the cuff kept getting longer. On his later visits to California he was talking more than ever, had begun smoking heavily for the first time, was putting on weight. When I moved to Colorado and saw him there, in Boulder, all these things had become extreme. But that was mainly surface. Inside, the same generous heart and mind never stopped functioning.

In 1977 he wrote a poem called "43," which was about his existence at that age: "no strange countries/no women/no dance, no clothes/still a wild & strange tune/a song that rises in the blood/not much blood."

Beginning with Kerouac's death in 1969 ("I felt like I got hit right in the head with a hammer," was how he later described to me his reaction to that event), Ted talked and wrote increasingly about death, the deaths of those he loved, and also at times of "laying down" his own "weary tune"—though of the latter he still spoke mainly in tones of comedy. A very serious, life-burdened kind of comedy, granted.

Death's sadness and grief, the "grief dance" of getting over a loved one's passing—these became all-absorbing matters to him, as the years went by. "The pills kept me going, until now. Love & work/were my great happinesses, that other people die the source/of my great, terrible, & inarticulate grief," he wrote in 1978 ("Last Poem").

We saw Ted several times in Boulder during his visits there between 1978 and 1980. The last few times we talked, he was usually in the same position, flat on his back in bed in the basement apartment of the Grove Street condominium where he was living in the summer of 1980—beard, books, belly, pills and ashes spilling everywhere. Crazy wisdom wasn't Ted's cup of tea, but it was buying that summer of his time: an escape hatch in the form of free housing for himself, wife and kids (Anselm and Edmund, Jr.) during those months when the heat in his home kitchen on St. Mark's Place got steepest. A couple of evenings each week he rose from his bed to teach poetry and fiction to East Coast white kids spending their summer vacations at this neo-Tibetan alternative spa in the mountains. The work load wasn't much, but neither was the pay. I got the impression Ted felt out of place in Boulder; even with its airconditioned nights, the town had no interesting street life or local culture, none of those indigenous emanations the poet inside the man could feed on. And the philosophy and tone around Naropa—a kind of bright-eyed suspension of disbelief, no jokes condoned—had little in common with his own. It was a sad declension for Ted, I thought. Yet there in the condo he lay, covered with the ashes of an endless chain of Chesterfield Kings.

His major interest of that summer was the slow passing of his mother, who was in a Massachusetts sanitarium, sinking under the weight of a cancer on her lung. Peggy Dugan. He phoned her every evening around six, burning up his pitiful salary on long, affectionate calls that were a moving thing to hear—his tone that of a young man talking gently to a sweetheart. I often heard, rather than overheard, Ted's end of them, because if I was in the house he always invited me into the bedroom when he was about to phone her. That's among the last memories I have of him, breathing with difficulty on his back in bed as the sun went down and the day got cooler—the evening was always Ted's morning—saying "I'm going to call my mother now, come on in and keep me company."

I moved back to California. Two years went by before Ted and I crossed paths again. It was at the Jack Kerouac Conference in Boulder—July 31, 1982—that I saw him for the last time. I'd stepped off an airplane at Stapleton, ridden with

Carolyn Cassady and Ed Dorn into Boulder, and within an hour was standing up to read excerpts of my Kerouac biography to a crowd of Jack's fans gathered in a Geography Department lecture theatre. The audience was large and mostly faceless as far as I was concerned, except for one hulking presence in the front row, off to my left. It was Ted, grown enormous, huge belly, big grey-tinged beard, prompting me along with encouraging comments as I read. Just like old times. (I flashed back to the time Ted had introduced me to my first U.S reading audience, at the Folklore Center in New York in March 1967.) I closed with a reading of some new poems. At the end Ted made his way slowly up to the stage—he had a bad foot, and was walking very gingerly—and gave me a warm greeting and friendly hug. We exchanged a few words, then the group broke up, and though we'd hoped to get together again the next day, it proved impossible; both of us were winging out of town again, in opposite directions.

Editing a series of books from Santa Barbara under the imprint Immediate Editions, I assisted in bringing out Ted's last book, *The Morning Line*. The final year of his life, though, I was in contact with him only by mail and telephone. I heard from friends about a visit of his to San Francisco, where he'd been given a hard time by some language-school people. Then later I heard of his troubles with some longtime friends in New York, petty matters that didn't sound worth the pain. Pain and suffering had crept into things for me also, over the years. Sometimes petty, sometimes not. I felt for Ted, I felt for all of us.

Then on the 5th of July, 1983, Ed Dorn called from Boulder and told me Ted had died suddenly in New York. No details. The next day Simon Pettet, a young poet who'd been close to Ted in recent years, called at Alice's request, and in a broken voice, provided the details. Ted had seemed "weary," Simon said, and had admitted, a few days earlier, that "last year was the worst." "Still," said Simon, "you thought he'd live to be a hundred." He was 48.

A friend from Buffalo, John Daley, one of the many younger poets who loved Ted deeply, attended his burial service, and wrote me a very touching letter about it. John told of how, at the military service on Long Island, a man had pulled the flag off the coffin, folded it, and handed it to Alice, saying "a grateful country and the President thank you." "Someone laughed," John reported, "probably [Ted's friend] Harris Schiff, and said 'Thanks for what?'" I'd ask the same question. One of the best writers of his time, and yet Ted's family couldn't afford to bury him in a private cemetery.

TED

Buried in the military
cemetery at Riverhead,
in the army plot,
a veteran.

20
PHOTOGRAPHS

OF BERRIGAN AND FRIENDS

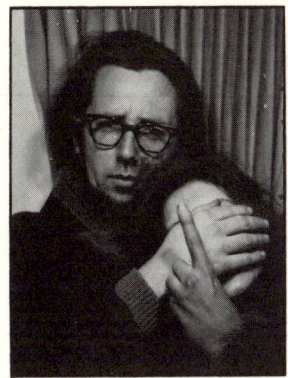

Clockwise from top left: Ted Berrigan with unidentified friend; Tom Clark and Ron Padgett; Anne Waldman and Lewis Warsh; Aram Saroyan (c. 1966–67).

Clockwise from top left: Peter Schjeldahl; Ron Padgett, Angelica Clark and Ted Berrigan; George Schneeman; Dick Gallup (at the Clark wedding, March 22, 1968).

Above: Angelica Clark and Ted Berrigan. Below:
Bernadette Mayer and Ted Berrigan (March 22, 1968).

Above: middle, facing camera, from left: Teresa Mitchell, Bill Berkson, Sandy Berrigan (33 St. Marks Place, N.Y.C., March 22, 1968). Below: Alice Notley Berrigan with Anselm and Edmund Jr., 1976.

Right: Ed Dorn at U. of Kansas, c. 1970. Below: Ed Sanders and The Fugs ("in concert" double exposure, 1966).

Above: Ted Berrigan chez MacAdams (Bolinas, 1971). Below: Tom Clark, Ted Berrigan, Ron Padgett (Ann Arbor reading, 1968).

Above: Ted Berrigan in Southampton (1971). Left: Berrigan teaching in Anne Waldman's class at the Naropa Institute, Boulder, Colorado, 1976.

Above: Berrigan and Waldman, 1969. Right: Ted, 1981.

LETTERS
OF TED BERRIGAN

[New York]
5 March 66

Dear Tom: your little Travel Diary just read itself to me, there were many little buzzes, you seem to have had lots of wait for all of them, so much for that kind of deliriuk how do. "deleriuk" is a rather interesting word my typewriter just coined, I'm sure you know as well as I do what it means.

Aram Saroyan had a wonderful letter published in the Village Voice, it was exactly like his poems and in fact *is* a poem: you shd publish it in thrice[1] : here it is:

Dear Sir:
Jack Newfield's attack on the English folk singer Donovan (Voice, February 24) confuses promotion — and the character of an audience — with the music.
Aram Saroyan
West 85th Street

Aram is a genius, there is no doubt about it.
Yes, I got *Once* & *Twice,* they were great to get & read, so intimate, just like

in life itself, and both good & personal (taste-wise) too, I loved them: please do include me in thrice or later if you like. I enclose my absolute latest unpublished poem, approx. the 5th in my new Jimmy Schuyler period (see MOTHER) tho this I fear is somewhat "after" Frank O'Hara instead. Praise god tho, its more me than them two boring poets as Ron Padgett might say if he read it there just before there. I have no copy of the Tulsa poem thats on the tape,[2] sorry, or I'd be glad to send it.

AGinzap[3] is bk in NYC after frolicking w/the Hells Angels all over gds creation, and I have a reading at Princeton (ha!) in Apr w/ him and John the Arse(bery)[4] and John Wieners. I guess I'll read "Song of Myself" just to show them I know something about life and grass and all that, too. what? More deliriuk!

I'll put in a couple of other poems too, they will make a motley lot, but maybe that'll be ok. One of the poems you sent me recently was really very nice, it was a run-on poem that changed direction a lot, I'll find it later and say more then. Must write my ART NEWS[5] jargon now, good to hear from you, best,

Ted

[New York]
[Summer 1966]

Dear Tom,

I have sent you 1000's of works in 3 separate envelopes.

Any you don't use please send back. Many thanks for Steve Jonas' works![1]

I am moving—new address: 286 2nd St. NYC. Life is sweet. Don't kick against the pricks.

The latest (Slice(s))[2] were stupendous. Also great.

F. Dawson[3] is an asshole, albeit a perfect one. James Joyce mentions LSD on page 52 line 4 or 5 of *Ulysses*.

Love, ted.

[New York]
[Fall 1966]

Dear Tom
   there sure is a lot I'd like to tell you but I'm awfully busy rereading AIRPLANE[1] which is marvelous!!!! Patsy Padgett[2] even likes it she says via airmail.
               I enclose my latest breakthrough into chaste beauty

                         yours
                       Ted Berrigan

   Harry Mathews[3] is here getting filled in on the scene by Roi Jones.[4] Did you know that bob dylans song ballad of a thin man was about roi jones? is it? tell!
                     I'm going to see and hear Japhy Ryder[5] read tonite. ps. Jack kerouac says i can come and interview him.
   Do you think itll be ok with george the jerk pimpleprune?[6] i am currently reading the thinking machine; encyclopedia brown, boy detective; color vision; the sea has found us; and poems of eugene field. last night i saw sea of grass at dick gallups. on nov 18th i am going to read at two high schools to pachucos and rape murderers and beautiful sexy cretin girls, for two c's. then i ll fix the capital bar.

                             love
                         edgar suet
                         TED

[Maine]
22 June '68

Dear Tom
       your kindly spirit floated in on a wave today, adding a sparkle to the rugged Island that is floating through my

consciousness like a breeze. I'm diggin my potatoes, and drinking a little wine. Nothing is uptight here but my typewriter and I guess Anne[1] is a little too, but Lewis[2] says he's gliding through it, digging this and being bored by that, yesterday he and Lee[3] were taking the garbage out in the rowboat to throw overboard and let the gulls eat, and Lewis tipped over the boat. They both got all wet, clothes on, this was at the very beginning of the trip, but they just got out of the water, righted the boat, collected the garbage, paddled out to the middle of the bay, and did the job anyway.

                    That's what its like here. We go to the well for water, get the wood for the fire from under the house where god has put an enormous pile of already chopped wood, come in the house, Sandy[4] cooks us terrific meals, David[5] plays all day with other kids, and doesnt come home for ten hours. Kate[6] catches little starfishes by the leg and brings them up to show me. I puff a few joints, have another pepsi, pee off the front porch, and thank god that I'm free white rich and enjoying all his good things in the world.

                    Then I read a few more pages of Chicago Confidential.

                    Everything is green and yellow and blue here, some days its many shades of gray, lots of fog.

    Tom, god will not be mad at you for living in a $12,000 dollar house. He has lots of them. Some people get them, some don't. You just enjoy it while you got it, and dont get too mad when ole goddy takes it away and sends you to the electric chair.

                Now I drink a little pepsi.

    Thank you kindly for the information about the latest Phil Whalen boke. I shall attempt to avail myself of it immediately. That gentleman is my favorite poet in the whole living world. Please convey my love to him, if you should see him, and I'd like his address mightily if you have it.

Have you ever read The Man With Red Hair by Hugh Walpole? Its an amazing SM scene book. Sandy is making a book full of many different kinds of dead flowers. Its a mystery to me.

Maine has many girls with fat-asses in it.

George[7] wrote me a great letter which expresses totally what it is to be a painter and not a poet. It said, "I'm sitting here smoking a cigar and drinking a pepsi and I look at the back of that chair and see that it's green."

       Write again, Love to you both
               Ted

           [Iowa City]
           28 Sept. '68

Dear Tom & Angelica too,
      hello. I'm really happy for you that you are going to have a baby. Babies do horrible and incredible things, but they are one of the ten greatest pleasures, and what can be greater than a great pleasure? Why don't you name it after me, I'm really a great guy, and I've always wanted a baby named after me.

        Tom, thanks for asking about *Clear The Range*.[1] I just can't bring myself right at this time to deal with that book in any way, so I guess it'll just have to sit in my bookcase for another twenty years or until I find some new kind of pills which make everything new (Ezra Pound pills).

        Iowa is actually ok. I drink beer and play pool at nights, with George Kimball (ha ha) but mostly with my research assistant (how do you like that?) an unbelievable guy from Texas named Henry Pritchett, who is a small guy with a mustache who talks exactly like a Texas Ranger. There is pot to smoke, a few pills here and there, it seems that every girl in the world carries a little bottle of dex in her purse, and things to do.

I have this private air-conditioned office, with secretary service available, a groovy desk, terrific bookcases and even a file-cabinet. File everything!

I'll enclose a few Iowa Workshop documents so that you can see what's happening. Some of the students here are good, two or three, and even more than that are good people. Maybe, if I think of it, I'll send you a couple of poems for the PR (subject to yr powerful displeasure of course), by a young ectomorph named Bob Harris, who, believe it or not, is Ron Padgett's cousin. He is very serious, digs Frank in a WCW way, and I'm a little impressed by him.

I wish I had something of mine for the PR, but alas, I write a poem a month, and they are 'beginning all over as if I knew nothing' poems, and so aren't so interesting. If I get anything good I'll send it ad hoc (sic).

Don't that make letters look interesting?
Anselm Hollo is here,[2] and is a kick. Wish I liked his poems. But I like him a lot, and we can talk. To Eskimoes. George Kimball is batted out of his skull, but is swinging on it as best he can. He threw a beer bottle through a tractor window the other night. Farmer Brown's cow stopped traffic for three hours on Main Street yesterday by just sitting. The Football players don't dig my hair and brains but they have to take it, otherwise George Kimball will beat the shit out of them for me.

I'm about to discuss one of your poems in my workshop, as you can see from the enclosed worksheet. Tom, I hope you'll keep me up on your poems, by sending copies, so that I can make a beautiful file for you in my file cabinet. Then I can spring your works on my students, and also know everything before everybody else, which is important ahem.

I got off the bucket a little there. Notre Dame whipped their own asses today with a little help from their froends. One thing a man dont need; a froend.

CHESTERFIELD

What's the gossip? Lewis MacAdams sent me a ripped-out-of-his-mind letter. Anne & Lewis³ sent me LEANTO by Ebbe Borregard, what a nut, but I dig him a lot. He is coo-coo.

What records are you digging these days? PS: I had already met CDB Bryan⁴ even before your letter. He's great. Very Edwardian, smokes pot every minute, digs The Traffic and Janis Joplin on his earphones while smashed, lets me ride his Shetland ponies bareback, takes the acid, and like that. By the way, POUND STERLING⁵ is genius, I re-read it the other day.

I miss Bernadette, Donna, Linda, and a few girls you didnt know about a whole lot. On the other hand, I've met ____, ____, and ____, and am working on ____, and ____.

It sure is fun to write a letter to you. PS: Andrew Crozier wrote me and asked for "a large selection of poems" to use in THE PARK REVIEW. Guess I'll have to send him fifteen copies of *American Express*.

Where is Larry?⁶ I want to write him but have no adress. He sent me a great picture of Eddie Bracken for my wallpp. (You got any wallpp? They only have them in Iowa).

So, warm & tender love to you both,
ted
The Splendid Splinter

PS: Write to me at the Univ.

[Iowa City]
2 Jan 69

Dear Tom
            your book[1] arrived today & what a great pleasure!
These old bones lit up like 42nd Street. I feel great. STONES
is beautifully outrageous as well as outrageously beautiful.
Not only that but it looks so real, like a real book of poems
by Donald Hall or Bobby Bly and then a slow double take,
swiss cheese, Apollinaire, the USA, Here's a kick in the ass,
boys, hurrah! Wow!

                                            Signed,
                                            Mandrake.

   Seeing those familiar poems, at least two of which I know
so well from conception to Military Service that I feel a
better than me me wrote them for me, gave me a few hearty
heart tickles in the pleasure teepee! Me cuckoo! Me flingen-
em in fasta boss! Heap Heap!
   The academy of the future is an undersea snowball
   I guess its about time now to talk like a bear and not like
a cigarette.
              The muse denies me words to speak of getting
STONES, but does not deny me stones. I drink a stone to
you! (drinks) that sure was good.
   I am in my office, Dick Gallup not fucking in the room
below, dont know what time it is, Indian break that pony.
   Enclosed is my anti-war epic in the manner of Denise
Levertov and James Wong Howe.[2]
                            By the way, HUNGER was
a wonderful book. I can easily see why Miller loved it so
much, and I loved it too, it made me so hungry I didnt ever
want to eat again, and then I did. (567 lbs).
   I have been reading Omnivore, The Biography of F Scott
Fitzgerald, What I Believe by EMForster, Grant's Memoirs,
The Works of Bacon (doodoo), a few bokes by Conrad, The
Origin of the Brunists, Life, Look, Columbia Record Club

Bulletin, the back of The Incredible String Band Record, a matchbook cover, and a toothpick. A dot. Nothing.

Here's a new word: spig. As in the eye is on the spig.

Another: Queel. Dig that queel. Or, I've got a little queel on my shoe.

Yours in Christ,
Dan Berrigan

[Ann Arbor]
[September 1969]

Dear Tom

Howdy! still don't have my typewriter fixed, so, few letters. Apparently yr reading here is set for sometime in the Winter (?) I think. The Big A, AG,[1] is coming soon to raise $ for John Sinclair.[2] The Trans Love[3] people are sweet. I enclose my latest photo. Many thanks for yr photo. Angelica is wonderfully lovely & you are pretty, too. Ann Arbor[4] is a wierd green place that closes at midnight. What the hell is there to do here? I read the complete memoirs of Ford Madox Ford & giggle. My students love me. Harris Schiff came to visit & read to my class w/ no shoes on. Hunce Voelcker also visited but didn't read. I like it here, when I don't have my cafard.

Love & kisses,
Ted

[Wivenhoe, Essex]
11 Oct 73

Dear Tom,

Life goes on in Wivenhoe,[1] despite few signs of it. We go to the pub for pints, dig the passing parade of senior citizens down High Street, & sometimes Alice[2] writes poems. Sometimes I do too, & sometimes I even tutor my tutees, by telling them it is all cool. They dig doing nothing plenty, but they definitely do not dig Henry James!

             I went to the dept. cocktail party this week, & met a few young pricks who teach something. One said, I've been told you're someone I should meet. & I said, yeah, who told you? which cut that gambit off. Actually these Literature Dept. Professors seem harmless to me, but I'm glad I'm not a student. It must take lots of pills to go to College here, for certain.

                 I met two students already who dig your works, one named Ralph who also digs Kerouac, Burroughs, Ginsberg, & not Henry James, & one named Simon who digs to be a poet not like Robert Lowell but like us, only better. Ha-ha! Who can do that?

  PS. (Now for the major point of this letter): It seems David Ignatow recommended me for a Guggenheim, & they even sent me the forms, tho they got here a few days before they were due back in.

           What can I lose, I heard my philosophical side mutter, & so with curt eloquence I filled in the forms, 12 copies of an account of the highlights of my career ("Once I sat next to Keith Richards at a movie, it was the world premier of Easy Rider."), 12 copies of my abridged bibliography ("Seventeen," plays written w. R. Padgett), & 12 copies of a brief account no a brief description of my project & its whereabouts.

            What project? At last I told them that my project consisted of me writing my poems as usual, including also new kinds not tried yet plus vast epics & etcetera. The place this project of mine could best be carried out, I said, was in N.Y.C. Heart-rendingly I added that I had been wandering the US & now England since 1968, teaching in Universities & raising family & all like that. This year I am having year abroad, but also teaching & working my fingers to the finger-bones. Now I feel a strong need to spend 1975 in New York City, among poets, painters, and big city culture so inspiring to me in my past. Only Gugg money could provide me with such a year, I pleaded, & also allow me to complete important projects with bigtime NY painters Joe Brainard & George Schneeman.

 I suspect strongly they will not buy my routine. But Alice would sure like a year in NY, and I could dig it I guess. The rest, old man, as you may have suspected, is up to you, Bob Creeley, Kenneth Koch, and Big Don Hall. Soon you will be contacted by Guggenheim agents and asked to speak on my behalf. No doubt half the poets we know under forty have already named you as a reference, Tom, but fuck 'em, I knew you before they did.

    Anyway, that's my most recent news. So far I dig it here, the pace is easy-going enough, and still I have plenty to do. Tonight I have to read The Scarlet Letter. Give my love to all the folks, especially to Angelica & John the Butcher.[3]

           Love & kisses,
           Ted

         [Wivenhoe, Essex]
         29 Jan. 74

Dear Tom,
   George Plimpton must have played without a helmet too often![1]

   But what a pity, since The PR was the only Poetry magazine in the world its size that was of any interest, not to mention that it was the best (poetry mag, I mean). Well, History will glorify you, in any case. Meanwhile, everyone not as famous as me & you (for example) will be fucked for a national outlet, not to mention no more NEW SPIRIT(S) or big glook masterpieces by Jimmy.[2] I am shedding a tear this moment for your departure from that arena, a tear of pure gelignite which I will send by letter bomb to George Plimpton on St. Patrick's Day.

Wivenhoe Park & its environs dig us, & I can dig it, but Alice yearns for bright lights, big city, &, as Keats so nobly did, for fame. (Ha ha, fame is great, eh, brother-member of the pantheon? it's like having a ry-krisp in your pocket when you want to play the juke box.)

Tonight I am going to read at Cambridge, for a handsome fee of twenty quid, & at Cambridge Tech too. I hope Lord Snow is there, I dig his novels & wd like to pop a few black bombers with him & rap.

The leaves of grass come slowly these days of few pills, but I have been scribbling in bed on a long tiny work, BIO-GRAPHIA LITERARIA. It is wonderfully no good, & mostly squibs, jibes, obscurities, & typical trivia from the cesspools of the NY School, for example:

>   Clark Coolidge is the Victor Hugo of
> The New York School, Bob Creeley the Pierre Reverdy.

and (further example)

>   DEJA VU
>   Discussing Max Beerbohm
>   with Mike Brownstein.

Pretty edifying, huh? I love it. Then, on the other hand, I enclose some libel about you I scribbled in a Mandrax fit of cloudy brilliance the other night. My awkwardness seems to be on the increase, with I mean which is a great encouraging sign for my future as a poet.

Your poems previously sent to Alice are beautiful & tough & tender & you are still the best poet of us all. (I do like Anselm Hollo a lot these days & hope you somehow got his book, SENSATION which if you didnt I'll send you, tell me). The ones, anyway, of yours received up to today make an unsurpassable & wonderful section in the magazine. Now, the splendors of JAPAN³ are here, & we love it, & Alice wants to print it, too, in the CHICAGO (European Ed. Nr. 2) which is almost ready. The first group in one part of the magazine, JAPAN separately in another part. OK?

This is the longest letter I have written in five years, and it is only one o'clock in the afternoon.

I await the axe from the Guggenheim foundation, due to fall in March. Bob (Creeley) wrote to tell me he had told them my works were of central importance to his own! Bless him for that. Kenneth⁴ said he would tell them I am culture hero of first degree, important poet, and phenomenon of considerable amazement. Don Hall said he told them I am so deserving he is speechless, plus oil. So, if they axe me, it will at least be pure, and not because I didn't get the proper forms & references. I am not hopeful, nor not full of hope, but it will piss me off for five minutes if I don't get one.⁵

I wish I could go to a Bobby Dylan concert. I wish I could see you & Angelica. & I wish our new baby to be either girl or boy, & not mutant-fish-monkey-cretin, like George Plimpton.

Love & kisses,
Ted

[New York]
9 Dec 78

Dear Tom,

despite a dexedrine & codeine hangover, & a tiny fly who doesn't know it's winter & so is flying near my left eyeball, I awakened this morning with a great surge of affection (not a hard-on) for you. I sold a few journals to Columbia U., & with the $$ we bought your really beautiful book, *When Things Get Tough On Easy Street*.¹ What a wonderful book, my god, it's so beautiful & tough & tender & not cynical, just hurt, like the song says.

Then, what further pleasure to have the Damon Runyon book[2] arrive in the mail from Harper & Row this morning! I might even buy a new pair of pants to celebrate.

So, my love to you & Angelica & Juliet & I'll see you in August when King Buddha summons me to Naropa to lecture on Speed & Poetry. I enclose a token of my esteem, TRAIN RIDE,[3] oh would that I were the "slick easy poet"! Love & kisses, Ted.

P.S. I read TRAIN RIDE at Bard College last night with the giant Robert Kelly[4] in the audience, & he boomed out many a hearty guffaw!

Also, did I ever tell you that I devoured Damon Runyon's works greedily in my early teens? Big Julie[5] and such names were my heart's delight, & when, in 1966 I first went to Lindy's for cheesecake with the Vice President of Clairol, I paid a silent homage to old Damon.

So, give my regards to the tree, Ed Dorn,[6]

& be seeing you,
Ted

[New York]
18 Dec 81

Dear Tommy,
    Love spurs us on, you & me, to only one death. That is why you can just call me "Laura."
    Hopefully, you are reading this after just having extracted it from a well-wrapped package containing:
- 1 Kerouac Compiled Other (A Collection)[1]
- 1 Mss. (poems) by me, to wit, THE MORNING LINE[2]
- 1 Mss. (prose) by Alice Notley, TELL ME AGAIN (her Autobiography, trad.)[3]
- 2 ltrs to R. Arons[4] saying publish these after sending one hun each immediately, any other profits later, as promised.

So, please ship Angelica soonest. Your friend, Ted.

PS: (which is the real letter to you)
 I'm loving getting all your publications and other signs of your phenomenal literary activities! Just like the old days, only we are crazier than ever, and more parts ache, too! I have a sore leg, a backache, my radiator's thermostat seems busted, and my wheels are less than rims now. Still, the mail must go through! But where did all these fucking Indians come from?, as Tab Hunter once said to Errol Flynn.
 Thanks to a small job of two weeks I was able to xerox and bind you your own spanking new Kerouac set, in red, to commemorate the Hollywood ten. In return you owe me one copy of your next hundred books, inscribed to me with appropriate apologies for continuing to write (it's a habit, I tell my students. While you are learning to make something, cultivate the habit as well, and you'll be a writer forever, if only out of sheer lack of willpower).
 I labored mightily on my mss., wanting something that would be like me, also a good read, also that it would meet "the requirements," plus amuse me, finally to make the thing. Eureka! It has continuities up the buttt, all of my Berriganism, some pretty good works, sincerity, plagiarism, enigma, and is capable of every page being subjected to strict new criticism even by Allen Tate himself, tho probably not by James Tate.
 The title is no doubt a phrase you are familiar with from seeing GUYS AND DOLLS, or from your daily calls to your bookie. However, I must confess that it evokes WICHITA LINEMAN for me, searching (not in vain) for another overload. Tom, I hope you'll do a cover, anything you want to do. I love what you did with Bob Creeley's book,[5] and your own,[6] too. I'm not so much interested in the illustration-y, as Joe[7] might say, but as Joe did say, a little bit of being illustration-y never hurt a drawing.

So. If you will deliver mine to Hank Aron, & if you feel like doing a cover, I'll be honored, like they say. And if you want to insert a page or three of drawing by you, I trust you completely to do it by feel so go ahead, and I hope Senor Arons pays you something to do that, too.

Alice writes in her note to Dr. Arons that you and she share an intense desire to do art wherever anyone will stand still for it, and so offers to do her own cover if he is standing still.

She also sends her love to you, and to Angelica, whom she will look forward to having live with us menage a trois as soon as you ship A. here. I send mine, as always.

Give my love to your neighbors.
Yrs in Serenity,
Ted

CODA: I too enclose note to Henry Aaron's brother, Richard, explaining that we send all to you because we are poets and so do not know how to send three separate packages.

Also: re: me. I have fans, as you know, and my bokes do sell. So, if AM HERE wishes to do an edition by me with handwritten poem plus hand-colored works by you, I think that if there were to be some modest number of those, such as ten, (?), for high price, ees more advisable than having fifty simply signed ones for a few pesos more. What do you think? Please advise (me) (and him too). In fact, I don't send him note at all, because this is enough typing, but please tell him thanks for his notes and invitation to me, and also that I plan to mention Future bks from this series in St. Mark's Newsletter, for which I am the leonard Lyons of book reviewers now. (January edition hopefully will plug your latest, plus Dennis (James Laughlin) Cooper's).[8]

Now, to bed, to read A Reader's Guide To Charles Olson, Biography of W.H. ("I took benzedrine")Auden, and, best of all, The Sporting News.

Got any copies of Shufflin' Phil Douglas?[9] I lent mine to Steve Carey, and so will never see it again.

"NEWSTIP", no. 1: Hot poet here now is Eileen Myles (to grab for future.)

NOTES TO LETTERS

5 MARCH 1966
1. The letter did appear in Clark's mimeo magazine *Thrice*.
2. Berrigan's poem "A Personal Memoir of Tulsa, Oklahoma/ 1955-1966," which he'd read at the Berkeley Poetry Conference.
3. Allen Ginsberg.
4. John Ashbery.
5. Berrigan was at this time writing numerous brief reviews of New York painting shows for *Art News*.

SUMMER 1966
1. Clark had sent Berrigan a copy of Steve Jonas' book of poems, *Transmutations* (London: Ferry Press, 1966).
2. *Slice*, an issue in Clark's mimeo magazine series (*Once*, etc.).
3. New York writer Fielding Dawson's work had appeared in *Slice*.

FALL 1966
1. *Airplanes* by Tom Clark (Brightlingsea, Essex: Once Books, 1966).
2. Wife of poet Ron Padgett.
3. America writer Harry Mathews, who'd been living in Paris.
4. LeRoi Jones, later Amiri Baraka.
5. Fictional name for poet Gary Snyder, used by Kerouac in *The Dharma Bums*.
6. George Plimpton, editor of *The Paris Review*.

22 JUNE 1968
1. Poet Anne Waldman.
2. Poet Lewis Warsh.

3. Musician Lee Crabtree.
4. Sandy Berrigan, Ted's first wife.
5. David Berrigan, Ted's son.
6. Kate Berrigan, Ted's daughter.
7. Painter George Schneeman.

28 SEPTEMBER 1968
1. The Berrigan cut-up novel, *Clear the Range*, later published by Adventures in Poetry/Coach House South (New York, 1971).
2. The Finnish-American poet, in 1968-1969 a fellow instructor with Berrigan at Iowa Writers' Workshop.
3. Anne Waldman, Lewis Warsh.
4. Creative writing teacher at Iowa, also a novelist.
5. Collaborative poem written by Berrigan and Clark, 1967.
6. Poet Larry Fagin.

2 JANUARY 1969
1. *Stones* by Tom Clark (New York: Harper & Row, 1968).
2. "Anti-War Poem," published in *The Paris Review* #46.

SEPTEMBER 1969
1. Allen Ginsberg.
2. Poet John Sinclair, then in jail for possession of marijuana.
3. A Detroit dope-poetry-and-music commune.
4. In 1969-1970, Berrigan was an instructor in the English Department at the University of Michigan.

11 OCTOBER 1973
1. In 1973-1974, Berrigan taught at the University of Essex, located in Wivenhoe Park, Essex, and resided in the nearby village of Wivenhoe.
2. Poet Alice Notley, Berrigan's second wife.
3. The butcher in the Bolinas, California, General Store.

29 JANUARY 1974
1. Berrigan's comment on the end of Clark's tenure (1963-73) as poetry editor of *The Paris Review*.
2. Poet James Schuyler.
3. Poem by Tom Clark.
4. Poet Kenneth Koch.
5. On 23 May 1974, Berrigan wrote: "Alas, the Guggenheimers told me a flat out cold N-O means NO. I was surprised."

9 DECEMBER 1978
1. Tom Clark's *Selected Poems 1963-1978* (Santa Barbara: Black Sparrow Press, 1978).
2. Tom Clark's *The World of Damon Runyon* (New York: Harper & Row, 1978).
3. Ted Berrigan's *Train Ride* (New York: Vehicle Editions, 1971), contains a section of funny negative characterizations of Berrigan's friends, e.g. "The whining Jim Carroll/the Snake in the grass Lewis Warsh/The slick easy poet, Tom Clark."
4. Poet, professor at Bard College.
5. Character in several Runyon tales.
6. Poet Edward Dorn was teaching at the University of Colorado in Boulder, seventeen miles from Clark's home in Nederland.

18 DECEMBER 1981;
1. A bound volume of xeroxes of periodical articles by Jack Kerouac.
2. Berrigan's final book of poems, published by Am Here Books/Immediate Editions (Santa Barbara, 1982).
3. Published by Am Here Books/Immediate Editions (Santa Barbara, 1982).
4. Richard Aaron of Am Here Books.
5. *Mother's Voice* by Robert Creeley (Santa Barbara: Am

Here Books/Immediate Editions, 1981; cover and illustrations by Tom Clark).
6. *The Rodent Who Came to Dinner* by Tom Clark (Santa Barbara: Am Here Books/Immediate Editions, 1981; cover and illustrations by Tom Clark).
7. Joe Brainard.
8. *The Missing Men* by Dennis Cooper (Santa Barbara: Am Here Books/Immediate Editions, 1981).
9. Clark's biography of Shufflin' Phil Douglas, *One Last Round for the Shuffler* (New York: Truck/Pomerica Books, 1979).

A limited hardbound edition of *Late Returns*,
signed by the author,
is available directly from Tombouctou

OTHER TITLES FROM TOMBOUCTOU
The Timing Chain, Douglas Woolf, 136 pages, 7.00
Phantom Pain, Lucia Berlin, 120 pages, 7.00
Convivio: New College Journal of Poetics, #1, John Thorpe, editor, 120 pages, 7.00
The Chest, Mohammed Mrabet, 100 pages, 7.50
Sunday, Phoebe MacAdams, 100 pages, 6.00
Neighbors, Stephen Emerson, 94 pages, 6.00
Beautiful Phantoms, Barry Gifford, 80 pages, 5.00
The Japan & India Journals, Joanne Kyger, 300 pages, 10.00
American Ones, Clark Coolidge, 48 pages, 5.00
Practicing, Jamie MacInnis, 64 pages, 5.00
Five Aces & Independence, John Thorpe, 120 pages, 5.00
No, You Wore Red, Michael Wolfe, 64 pages, 5.00
Wild Cherries, Dale Herd, 88 pages, 5.00
Shit On My Shoes, Duncan McNaughton, 120 pages, 5.00
This Eating & Walking, Leslie Scalapino, 56 pages, 3.00
The Air's Nearly Perfect Elasticity, Richard Duerden, 118 pages, 3.50
Shameless, Jim Gustafson, 64 pages, 3.00
The Basketball Diaries, Jim Carroll, 156 pages, 4.00
How I Broke In, Tom Clark, 80 pages, 3.00
Stories & Poems, Gailyn Saroyan, 48 pages, 2.25
Frenchy & Cuban Pete, Bobbie Louise Hawkins, 80 pages, 3.00
Sumeriana, Duncan McNaughton, 80 pages, 3.00
FIVE, Lawrence Kearney, 80 pages, 3.00
News from Niman Farm, Lewis MacAdams, 48 pages, 2.50

DESERT ISLAND CHAPBOOK SERIES
New York Notes, Stephen Ratcliffe, 24 pages, 3.00
Start Over, Bill Berkson, 32 pages, 3.50
Let Us Not Blame Foolish Women, Dotty leMieux, 24 pages, 3.50
Triggers, Donald Guravich, 32 pages, 3.50